Day 1 – This is the day I officially arrived in the morning.

Since this was a short stay in Iceland, I really wanted to hit the ground running. More importantly, I wanted to avoid jetlag, so I decided to take a tour of the City of Reykjavík. It was not a long tour, no more than 3 or so hours, but it was enough to keep me awake and see some of the places which were on my list. As part of the tour, I visited the following landmarks in an attempt to learn about Reykjavík's beginnings as a fishing village to what is now a modern capital.

Pearl (Perlan)

This dome-shaped, glass building was designed by Ingimundur Sveinsson and is supported by six massive hot-water tanks - each with a capacity of 4 million liters (over 1 million US gallons). The dome houses an observation platform offering panoramic views of the city and its surroundings.

Quite a bit was under construction inside the museum at the time I visited, so I decided to head out to the observation deck, and took an image of the all glass dome of the Pearl:

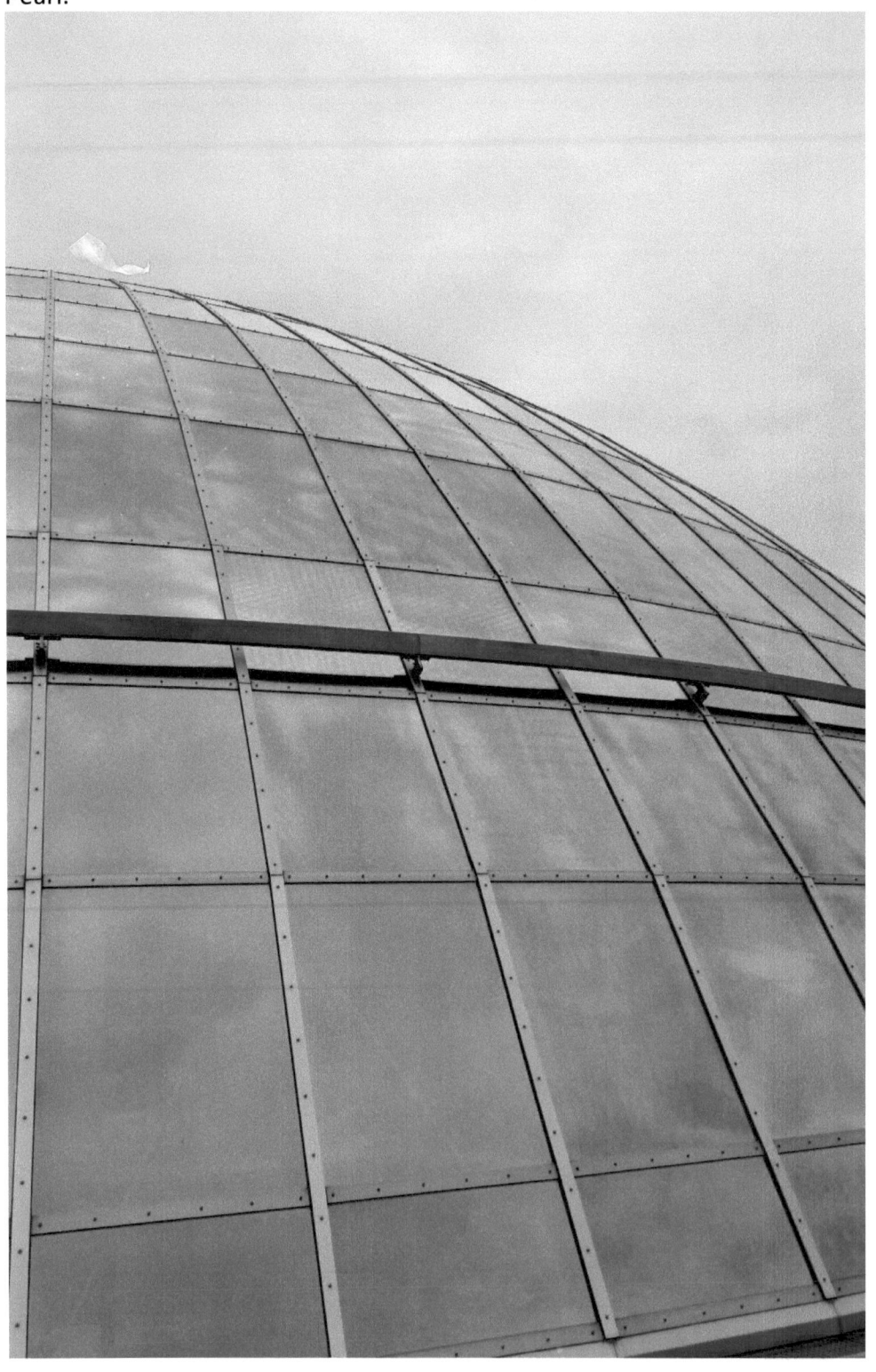

Here are views of the city and surrounding areas while standing on the observation deck of the Pearl:

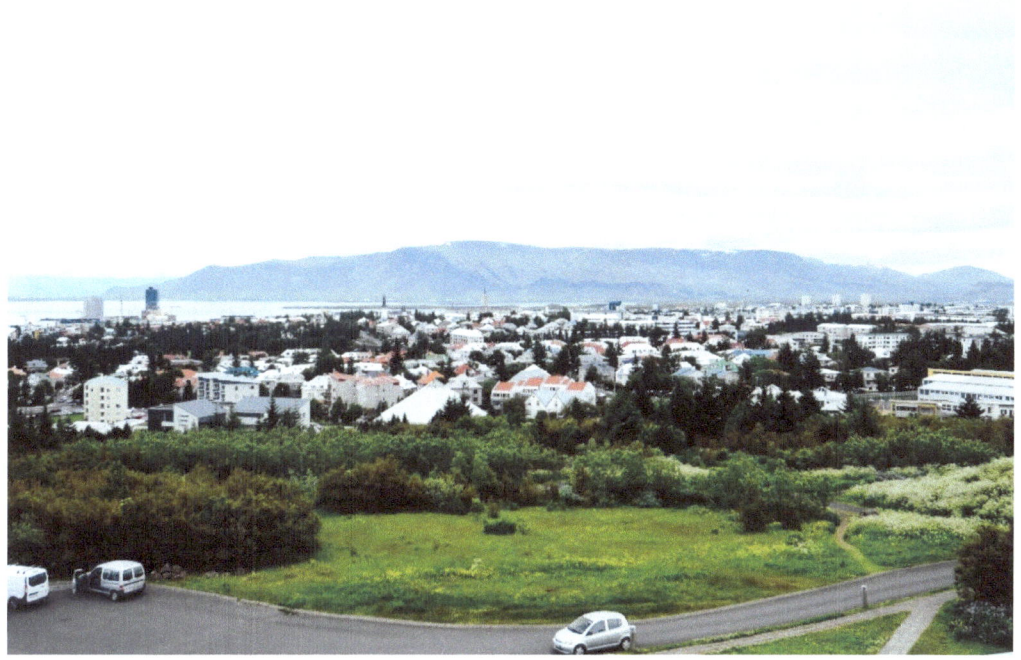

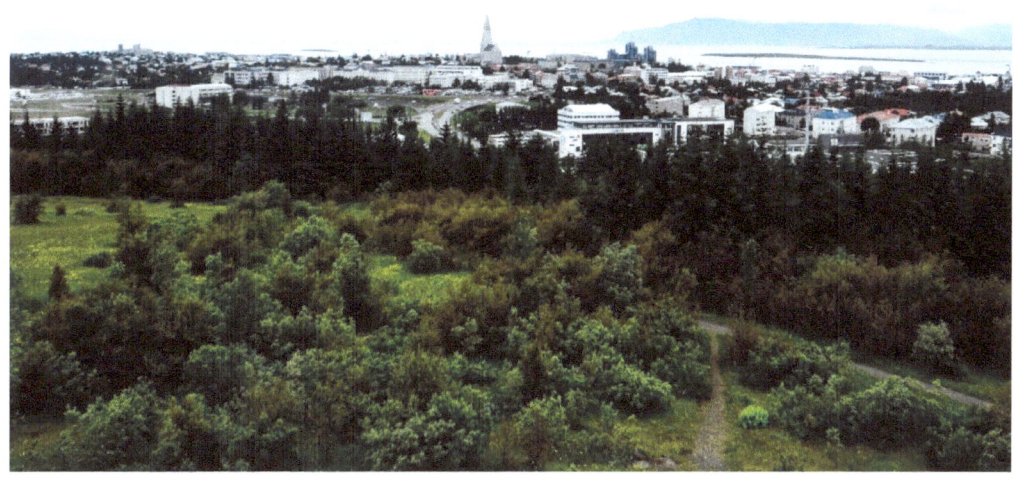

I found the interior of the dome more interesting than the exterior:

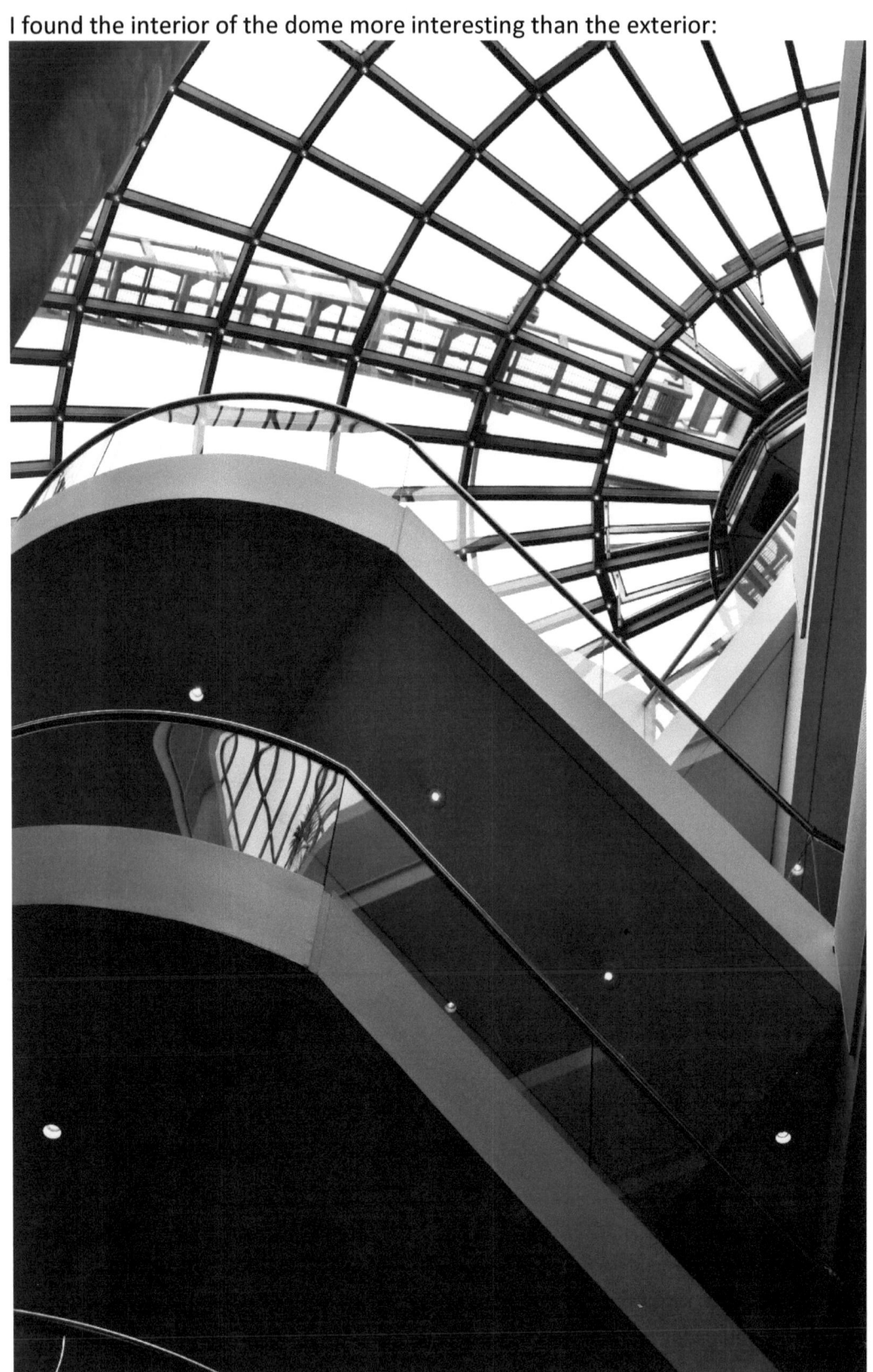

Just outside Pearl is Torbjorg Palsdottir's creation of some sculptures of Jazzmen playing musical instruments. These were created in the 1970s.

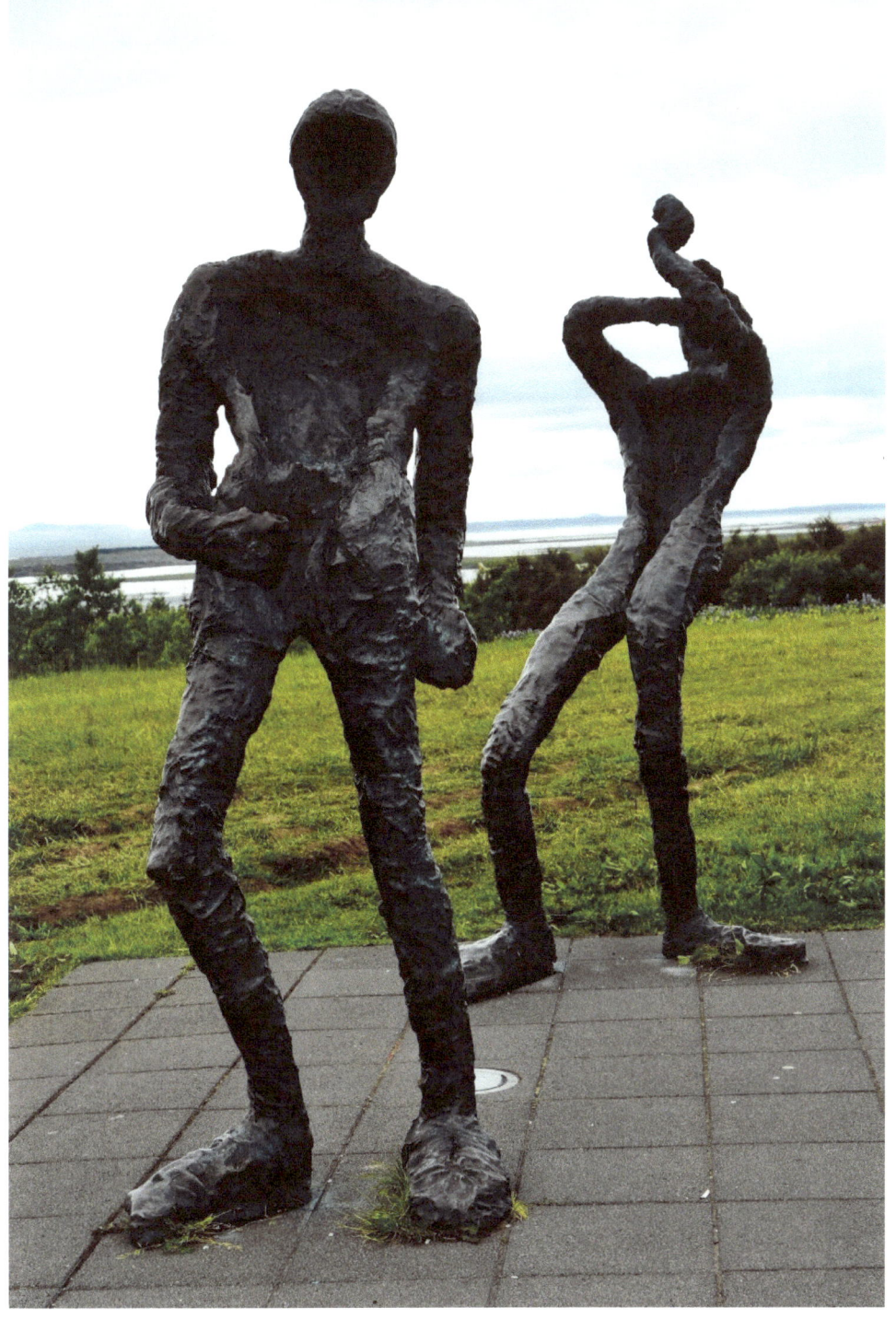

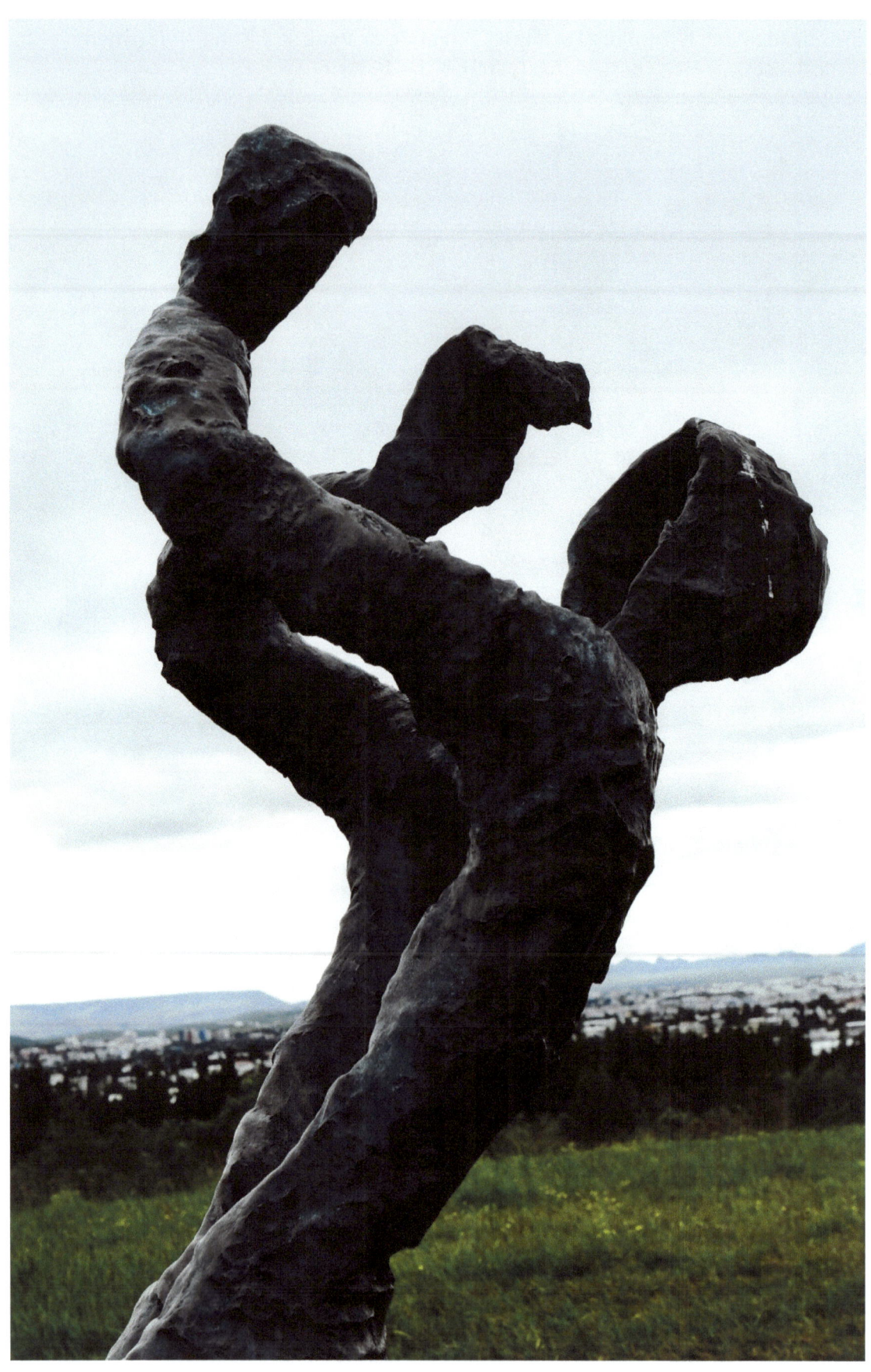

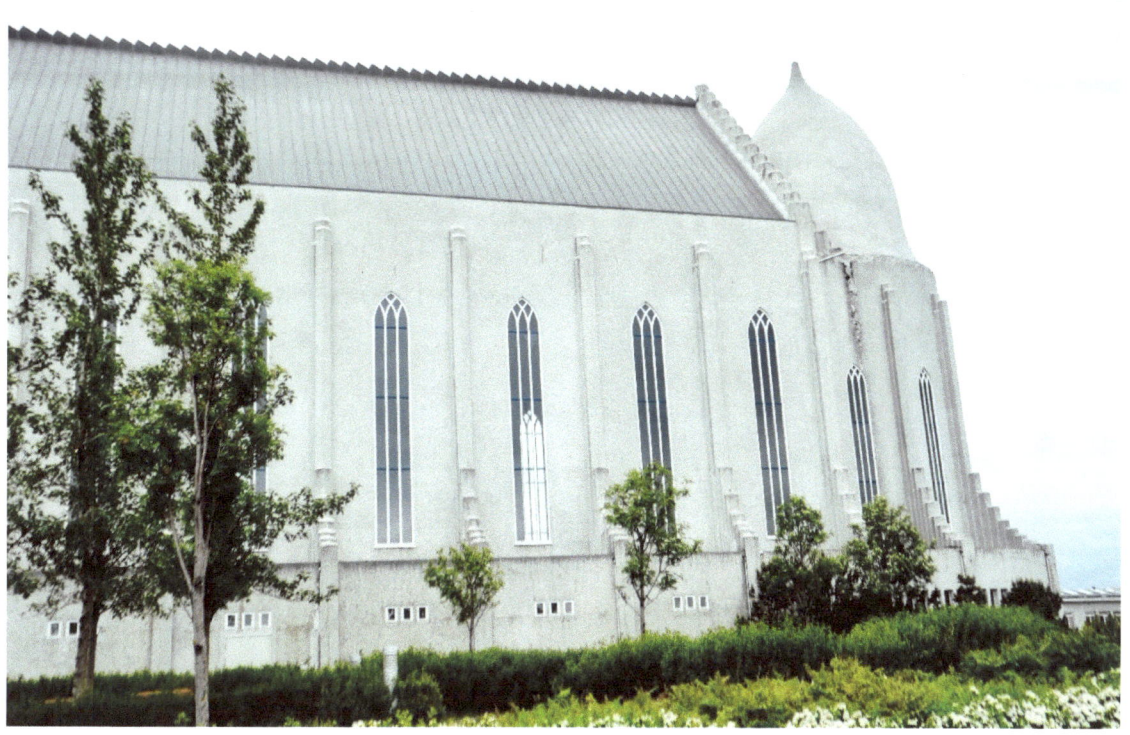

The church features a gargantuan pipe organ designed and constructed by the German organ builder Johannes Klais of Bonn. Standing tall at an impressive 15m (49ft) and weighing a remarkable 25 tons, this mechanical action organ is driven by four manuals and a pedal, 102 ranks, 72 stops and 5275 pipes, all designed to reproduce powerful notes capable of filling the huge and holy space with a range of tones - from the dulcet to the dramatic. Its construction was completed in December 1992 and has been utilized in a variety of recordings, including some by Christopher Herrick. I wish I could have listened to someone playing it. I am sure it would have sounded as impressive, if not more than what it looks like.

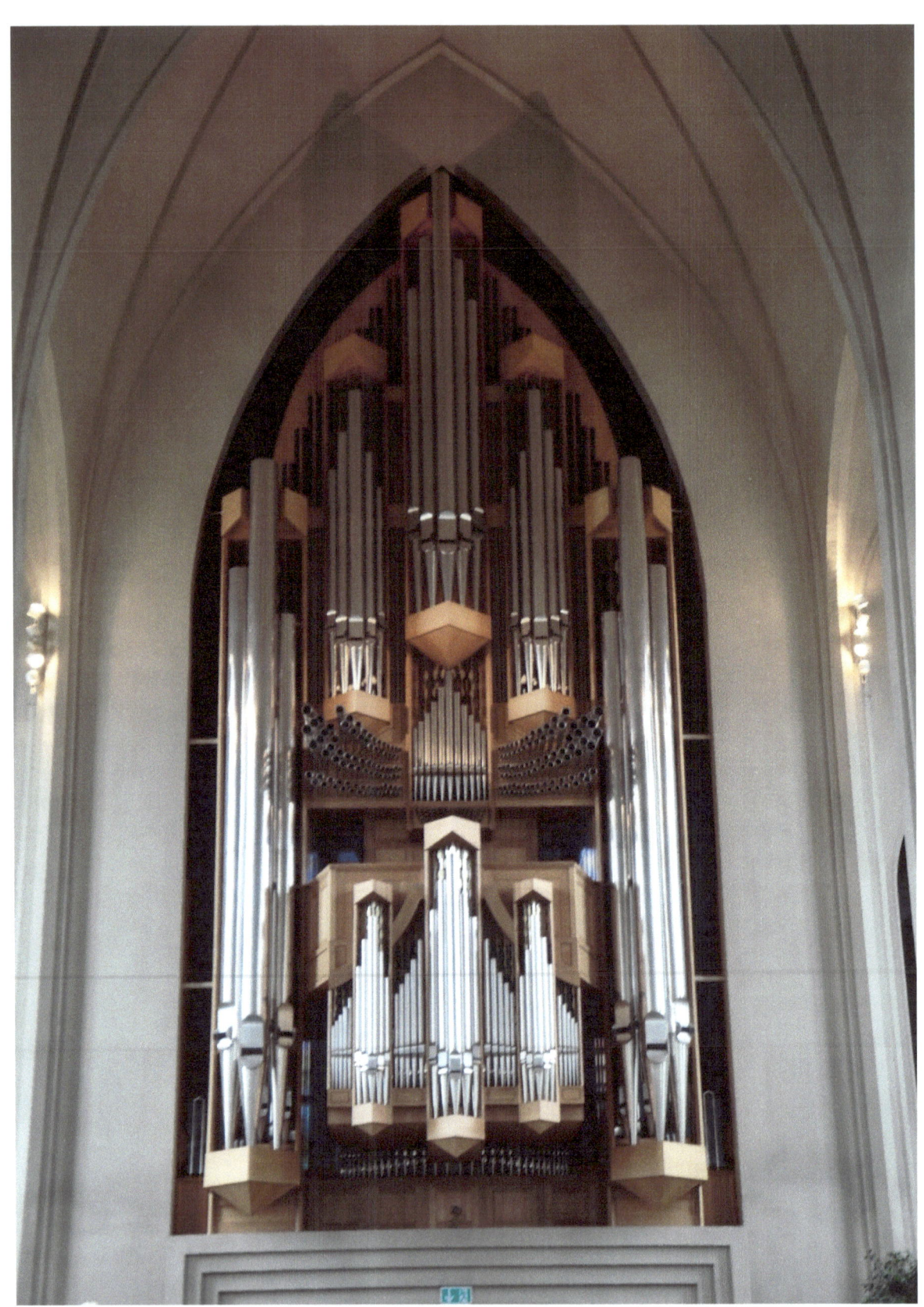

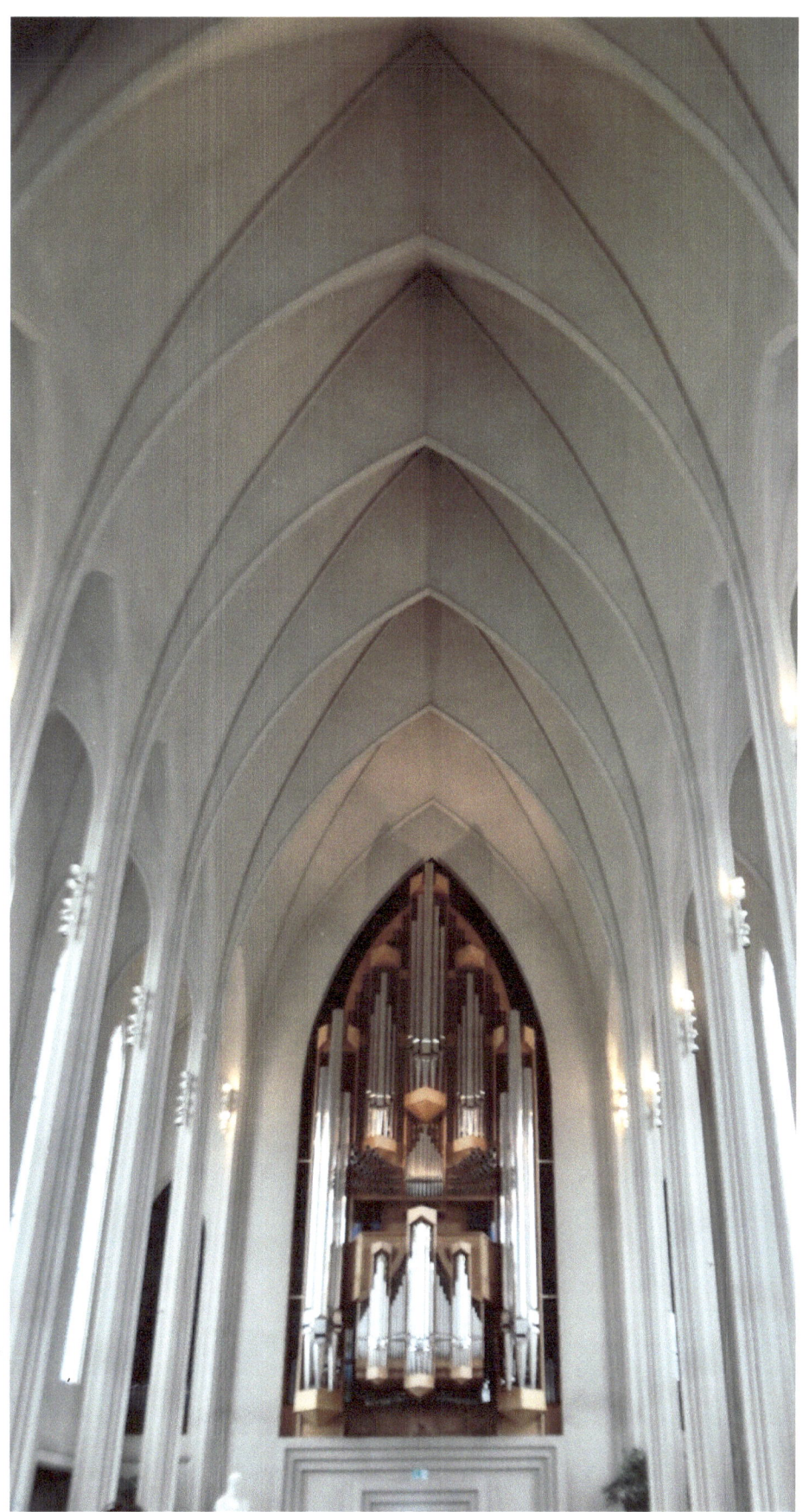

Standing directly in front of the church, and predating it by 15 years, is a fine statue of Leifur Eiriksson (c. 970 – c. 1020) – the first European to discover America. Records suggest that Leifur landed on the shores of the new world in the year 1,000 A.D., that's 500 years before Christopher Columbus. The statue, which was designed by Alexander Stirling Calder, was a gift from the United States in honor of the 1930 Alþingi Millennial Festival, commemorating the 1,000th anniversary of the establishment of Iceland's parliament at Þingvellir in 930 AD. Sorry, I was not able to take a good picture of this figure ☹.

Harpa Concert Hall and Conference Center

This had its opening concert on May 4, 2011. The building features a distinctive colored glass facade inspired by the basalt landscape of Iceland. This shot of Harpa is was taken from the marina (it's the black building, back right):

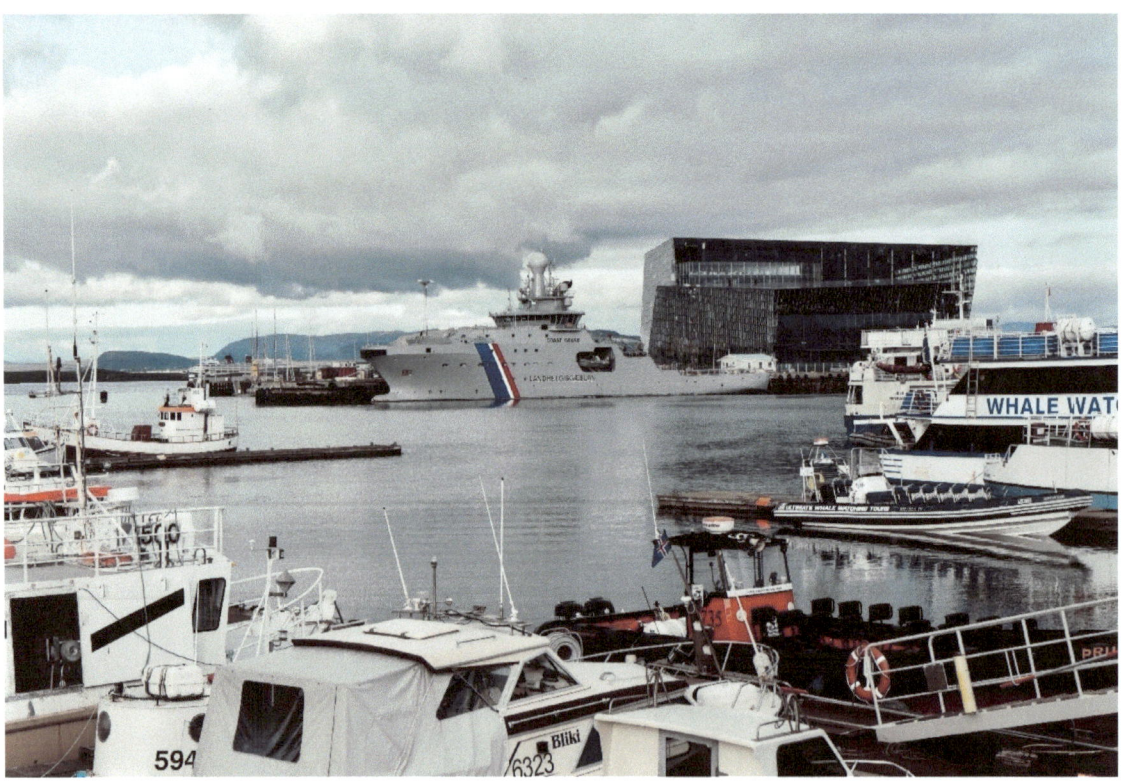

The marina itself is a nice place to visit. The tour did not stop here, but just drove us in to show its location. I returned the next day as I took a stroll after I had dinner at one of the restaurants located right by the pier.

Since there is a military ship in this shot, I thought I would bring up that Iceland has no army; it does however have a coast guard. One of the reasons is the number of inhabitants in Iceland. I hear differing numbers from different resources, but it is about 340,000 inhabitants of which a little over a third live in Reykjavík. From this marina area, there are a few tours which head out to the waters. There are options for whale watching and puffin tours (amongst other options).

I am now going to bring up a little political history with Höfði house.

It is best known as the location for the 1986 Reykjavík Summit meeting of Presidents Ronald Reagan of the United States and Mikhail Gorbachev of the Union of Soviet Socialist Republics.

Höfði was built in 1909 and is located at Félagstún. Initially, it was built for the French consul Jean-Paul Brillouin in Iceland and was the exclusive residence of poet and businessman Einar Benediktsson (1864-1940) for many years. That effectively was a step to the end of the Cold War. Within the building, the flags of the United States and the Soviet Union are cross-hung to commemorate the meeting. In the 1940s and 1950s, it was home to the British Embassy in Reykjavík. The city of Reykjavík purchased the house in 1958 and restored it to its former glory. It's now used for formal receptions and festive occasions. We did not have the opportunity to go inside, unfortunately.

But then tragedy struck!!!! September 25, 2009, on the building's 100th birthday, Höfði was damaged in a fire. All irreplaceable artifacts were luckily saved.

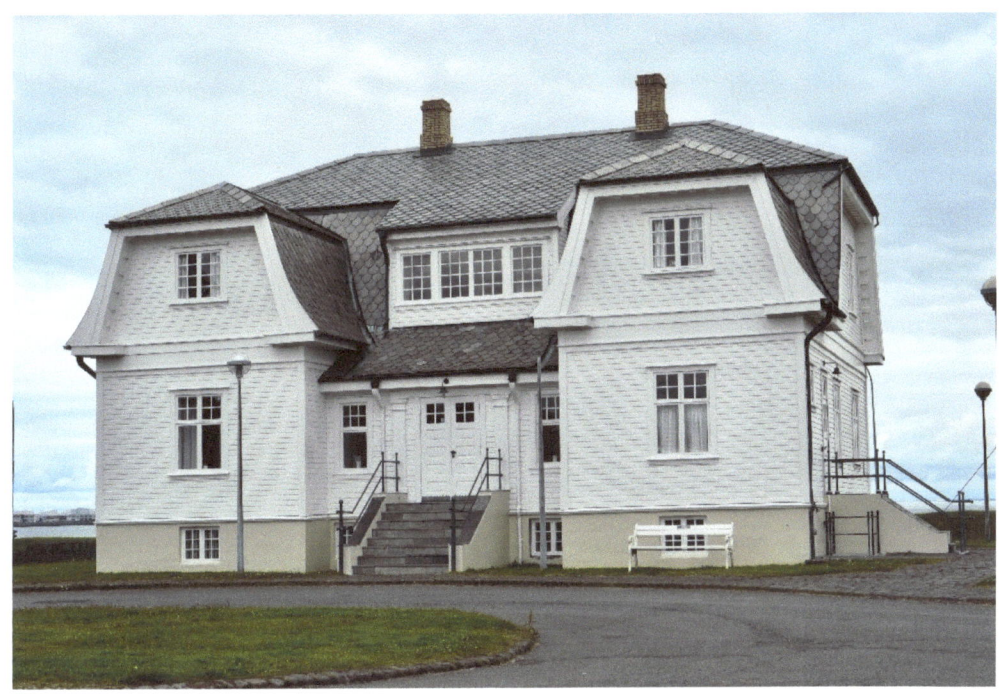

The last stop was at a structure just by the water. I had to be careful when taking the shot, as there was a bike and walking path behind where I was standing. Iceland has many of these paths as the locals use biking as a way of transit. The bikers are rather aggressive and can come up on you fast and I was nearly run over. Thank goodness for people telling (yelling rather) me to get out of the way when I was trying to take the shot.

The name of this structure is "Solfar Sun Voyager." I thought it looked like a Viking Ship, but it is really an ode to the sun.

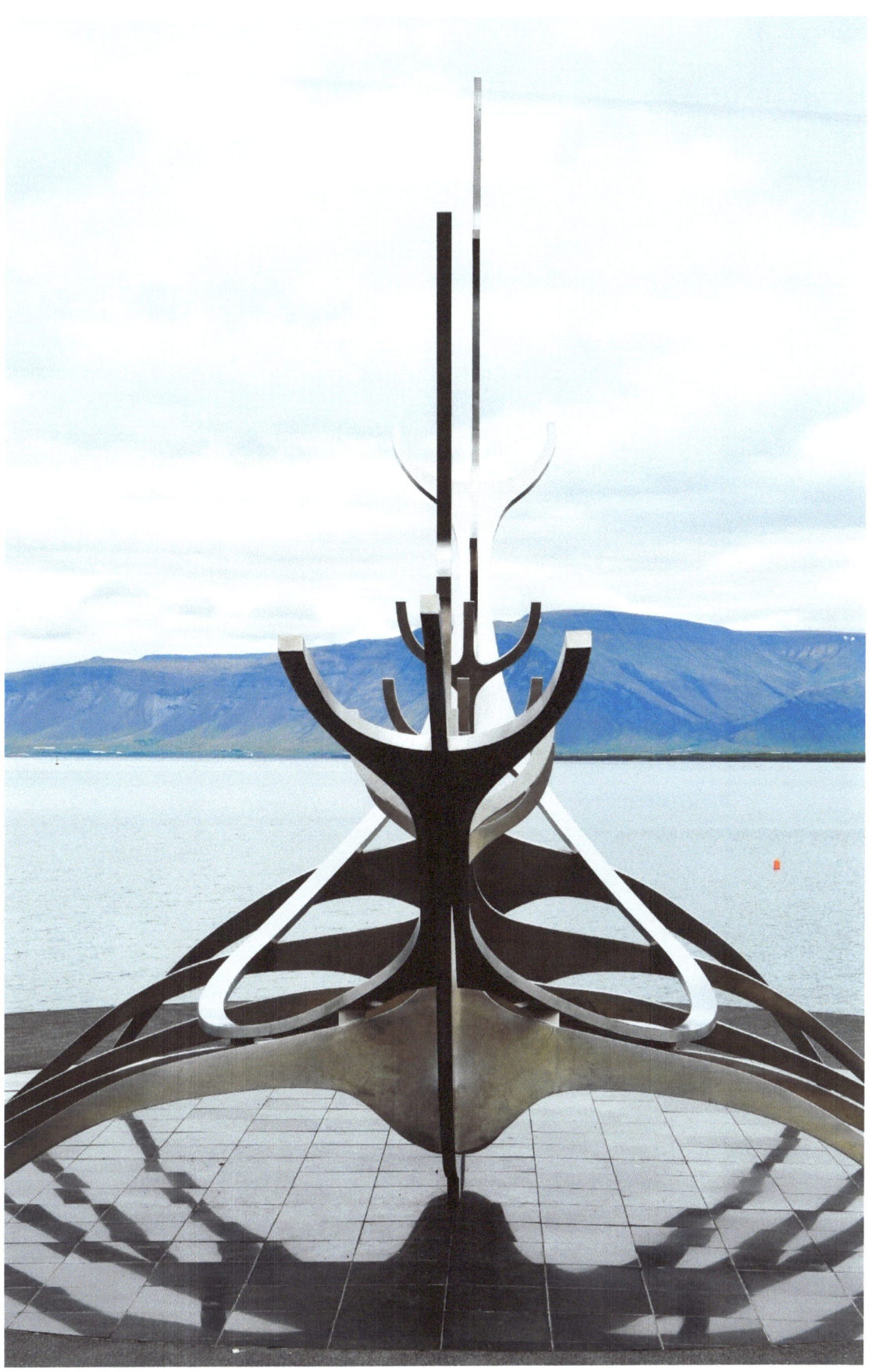

Day 2

This was a late start day to The Blue Lagoon, which is about an hour's drive from Reykjavík. You are probably wondering what the significance of the Blue Lagoon is. Well, let me tell you. It's a natural pool of mineral rich geothermal water and is located in the middle of a lava field in the Icelandic wilderness. The Lagoon is a combination of mineral-rich fresh and sea water of 38-43°C (100-110°F), surrounded by magnificent mountain ranges. It is ideal for enjoying the views, wading and soaking in the shallow 3-5 foot waters, while the air temperature typically ranges from 3 to 13°C (25-55°F). I am not a swimmer so I didn't actually go swimming. I just stuck my feet in the water and relaxed. It was easy to slow down while there. There are actually benefits to the thermal waters due to the silica present. It has been known to help those with psoriasis.

Luckily, I booked the spa/pool portion before I arrived in Iceland. As I walked in to the spa/geothermal pool area, people without tickets were being turned away as they were already sold out. Regardless, even if not entering the spa/geothermal pool area, it is a place to see, as there are trails that go around the lava rock areas, and views of the geothermal power plant.

Some of the views of the water from the trails:

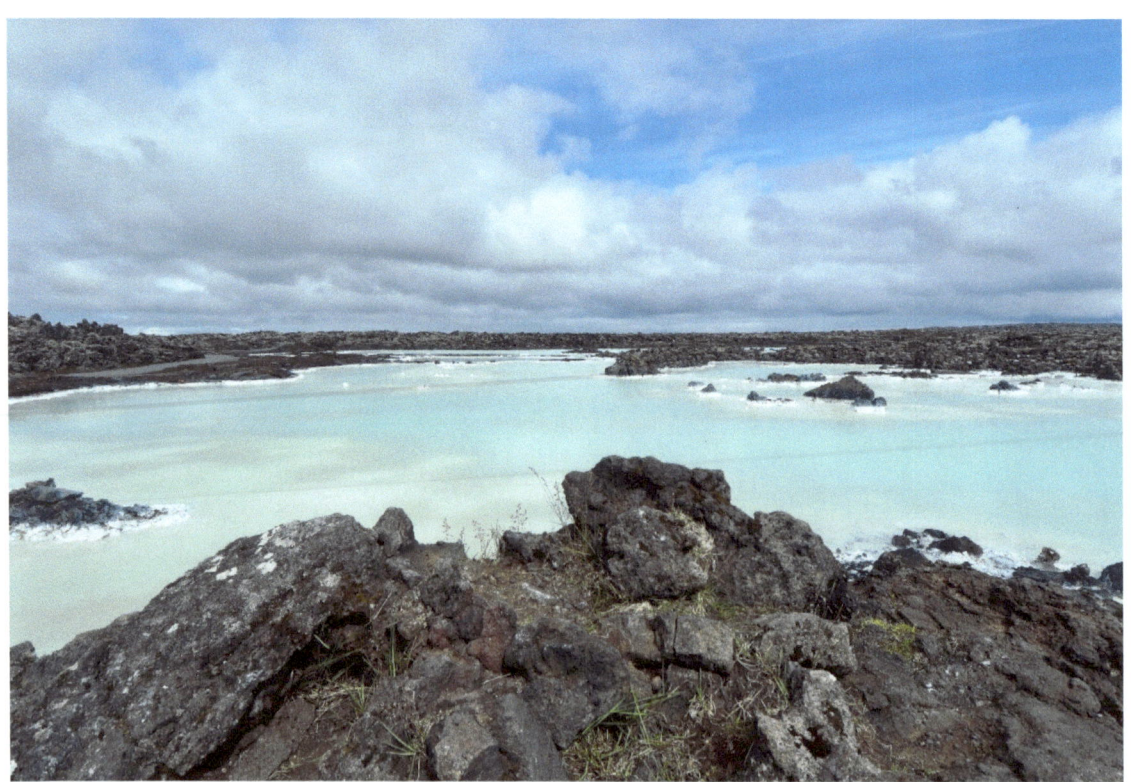

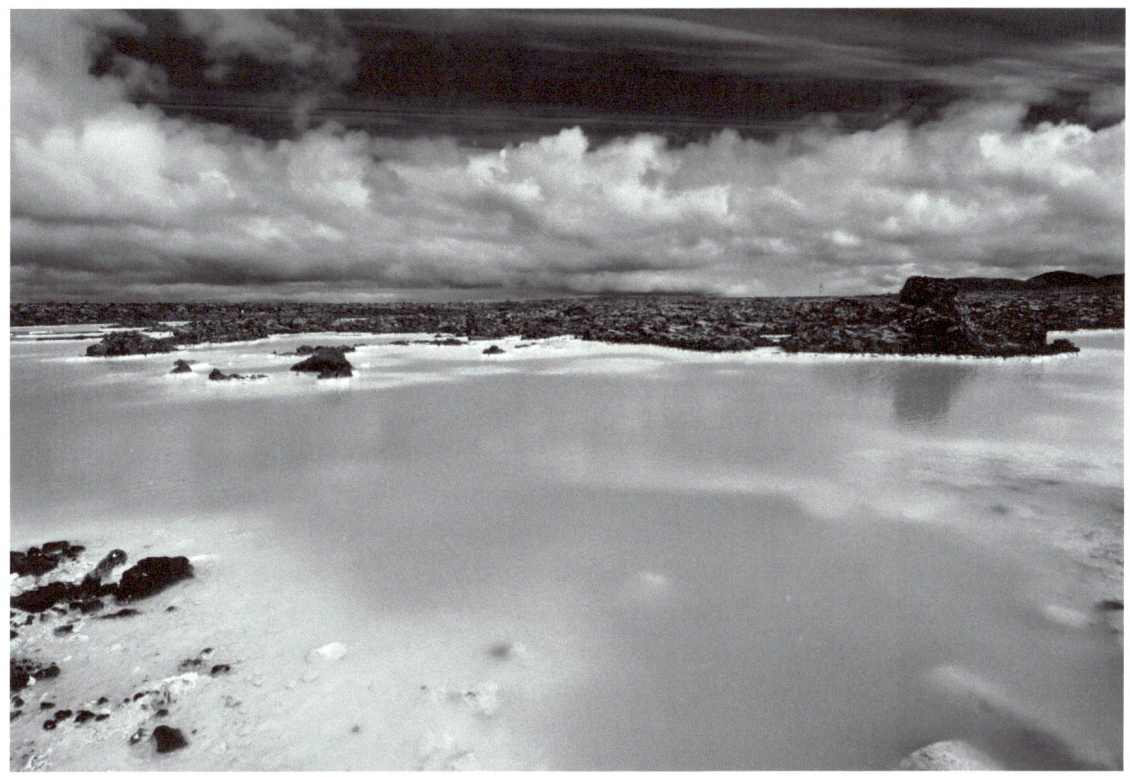

The Terrain:

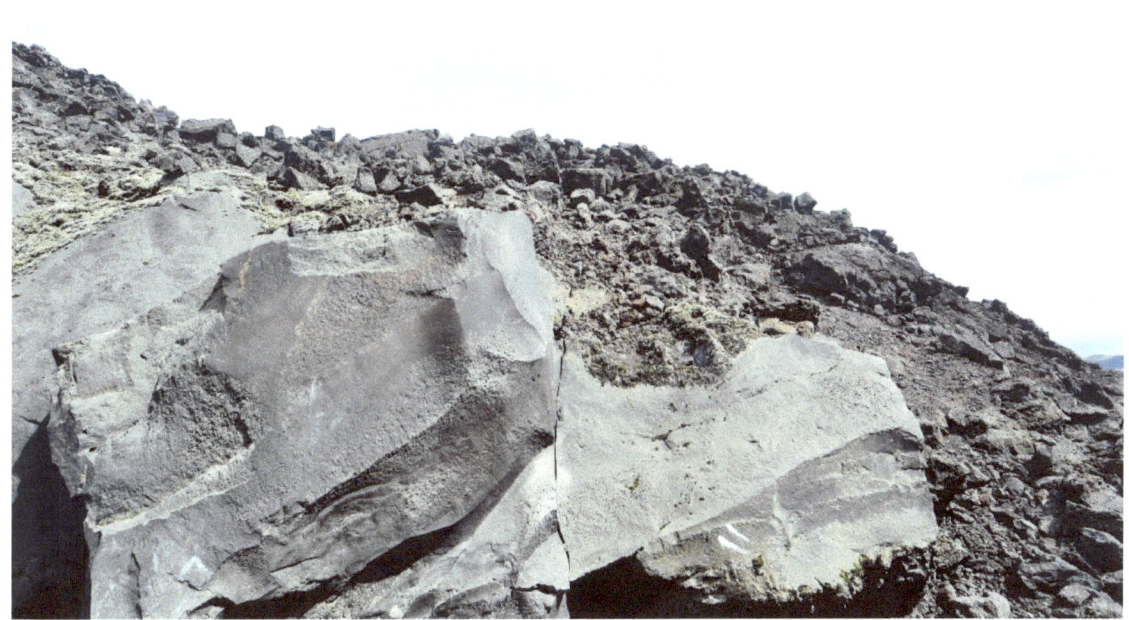

Day 3
This was the last full day of my trip.

I decided to take the Golden Circle tour, which although touristy, shows some of Iceland's most popular attractions including the country's natural, cultural, and historic sites. From Reykjavík, the Golden Circle tour took me right up to Thingvellir National Park, Gullfoss Waterfall, and geyser geothermal area.

Thingvellir National Park is a UNESCO World Heritage site where the tectonic plates of Europe and North America meet and one of the world's oldest parliaments was founded in 930 AD. Thingvellir National Park was founded in 1930, marking the one-thousandth anniversary of the Althing. The park was later expanded to protect the diverse and natural phenomena in the surrounding area, and was designated as a World Heritage Site in 2004. While at Thingvellir, I had the opportunity to take some shots of the fissures resulting from the shifting tectonic plates. This is an area where the North American and European plates meet and move at about the rate of 2cm per year. Yes, I effectively was on 2 continents without leaving the country!

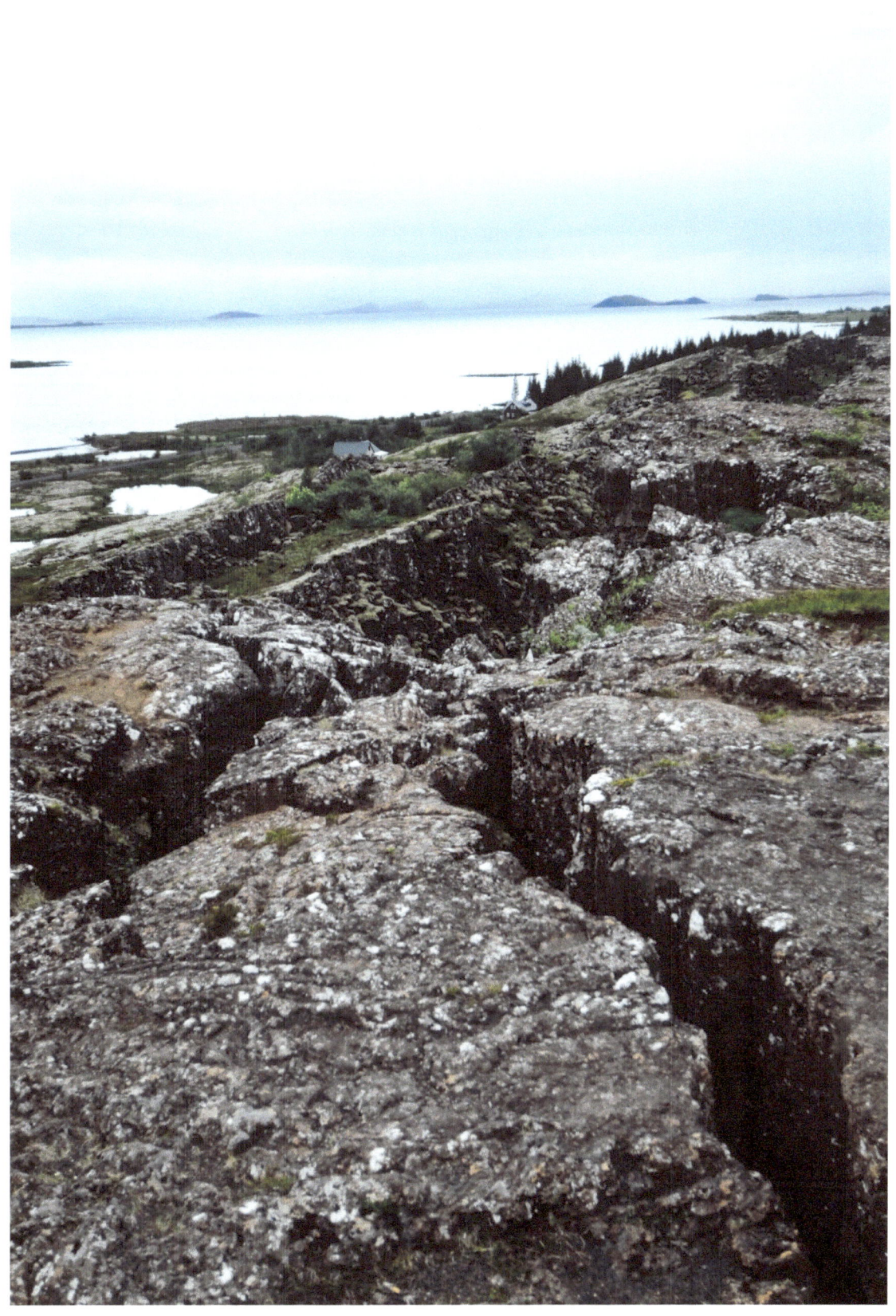

Then I moved on to the Gullfoss waterfall, the queen of Iceland's waterfalls, tumbling down a deep gorge. Gullfoss translates to "Golden Falls" and is one of Iceland's most beautiful and is Iceland's most popular waterfall. Gullfoss is in the river Hvítá (in English: white river), which has its origin in the glacier lake Hvítávatn (in English: white river lake) at Lángjökull glacier about 40km (25 miles) north of Gullfoss. Glacial water is brownish, since it carries lots of sediments that the glacial ice has carved off the earth. Gullfoss is called the "Golden Falls," since on a sunny day the water plunging down the three-step staircase and then tumbling in two steps down into the 32 m (105ft) deep crevice truly looks golden. I did not capture that as you can see this day is overcast. So, the green from the moss and wildflowers are showing off here. To stand at Gullfoss and wallow in the beauty and the wonder of nature was an uplifting experience. I was feeling more energetic and refreshed when leaving Gullfoss than when I arrived. Perhaps it was that chilly mist which came up from the crevice of the falls or the power of rushing water had as it approached the falls.

There are multiple platforms where the falls can be seen; I went to the lowest portion, which took me closer to the actual falls. If you look really closely, you can see people at the upper level. The mist is kind of hiding them.

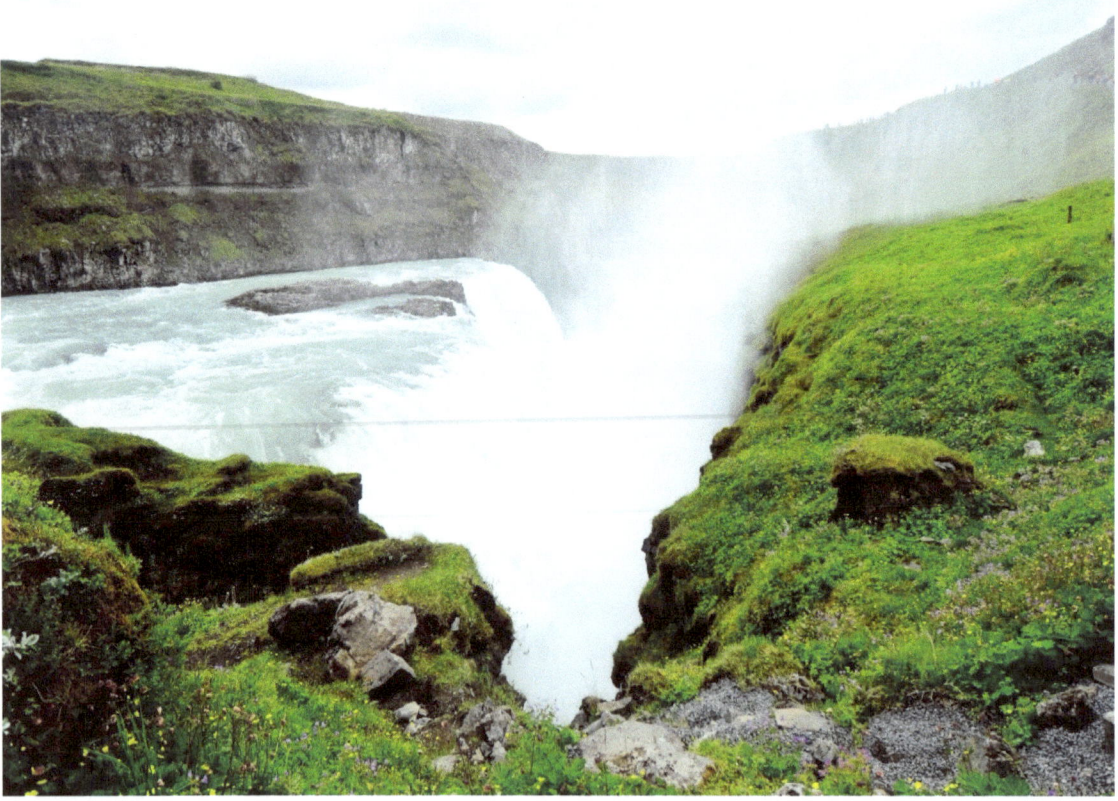

Want to hear a story regarding Gulfoss? Of course, you do and it goes like this:

> Sigríður Tómasdóttir was the daughter of Tómas Tómasson who owned the waterfall in the first half of the 20th century. She lived at a farm nearby and loved Gullfoss as no one else could. At this period of time there was speculation about using Gullfoss to harness electricity. Foreign investors who rented Gullfoss indirectly from the owners wanted to build a hydroelectric power plant, which would have changed and destroyed Gullfoss forever. Sigríður Tómasdóttir was the one that protested so intensely against these plans by going as far to threaten that she would throw herself into Gullfoss and thereby kill herself. To make her threat believable, she went barefoot on a protest march from Gullfoss to Reykjavik. Roads at that time weren't paved and when she arrived after 120 km (75 miles), she was in very bad shape - her feet were bleeding! The people believed her and listened and the power plant at Gullfoss was never built.

Today, one can see the memorial site of Sigríður that depicts her profile at the top of the falls and can be seen on the drive to the falls.

The next stop was the geyser geothermal area, home of the famous Geyser and Strokkur hot springs. The Strokkur hot spring erupts every 5 minutes or so, making it one of the most active geysers. There are more mini geysers in the area, which don't "spout," just bubble. Now, back to Strokkur. Strokkur (the churn) is currently the most energetic spouting spring in Iceland. It spouts every few minutes, sometimes to a height of 40 m (131 ft.), yet generally less than 10-20 m (33 - 66 ft). Be careful where you stand, in particular on windy days, as the water temperatures are quite hot - generally between 80 and 100°C (176-212°F).

Strokkur:

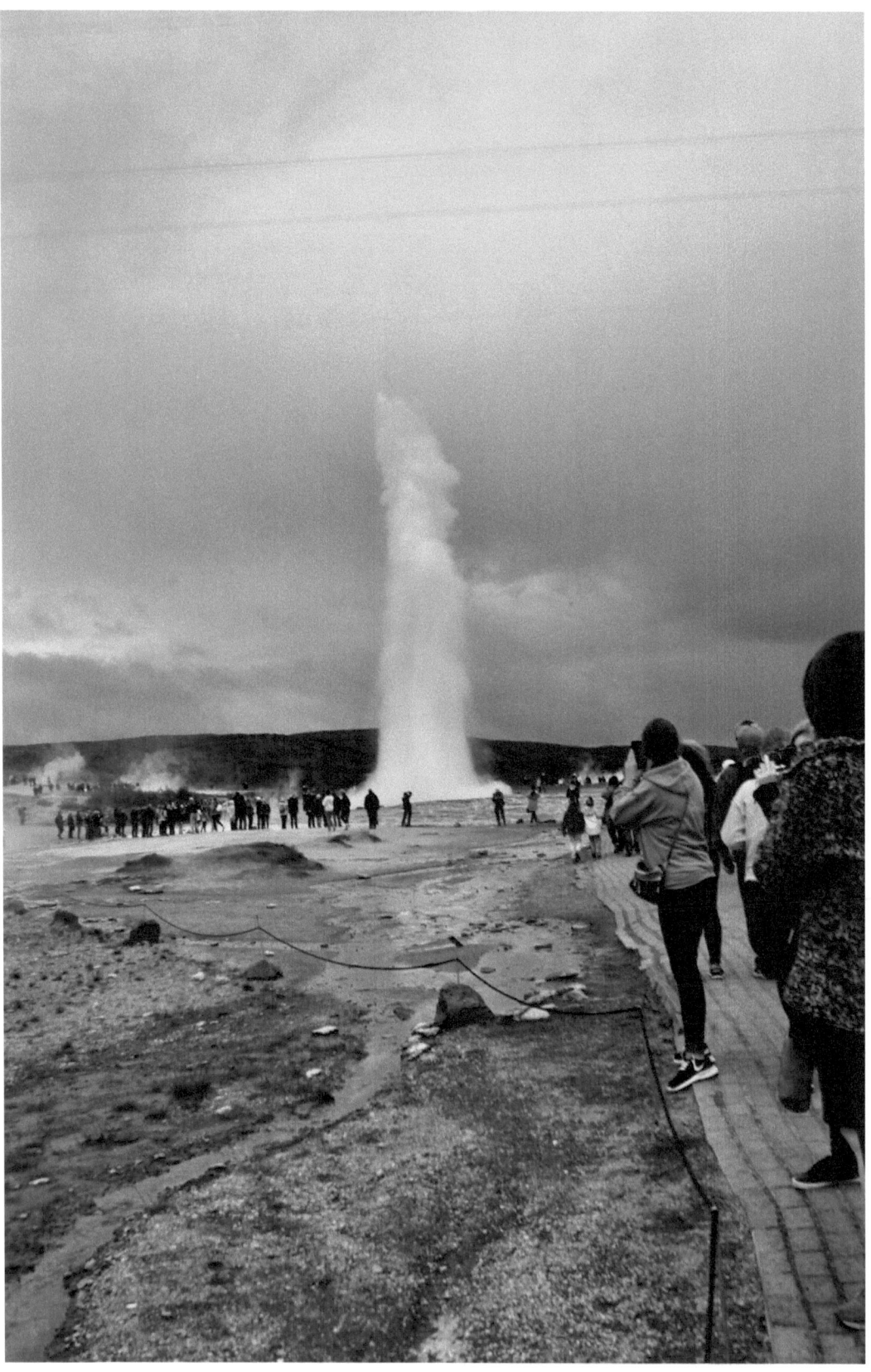

There are ropes set off so people don't go past a defined path. Notice the low laying rope in the photo. The ground is wet and they want restricted movement near the, even small, geysers for safety reasons. I saw a small, curious child wanting to cross; luckily her mother stopped her! ;)

Thus far, little is known of Strokkur's age and history. It was set off during an earthquake in 1789, having then been quiescent for some time. In all probability though, it had been active before. The year after Strokkur started to spout, it was extremely powerful and ejected water, gas and steam with tremendous force. Towards the beginning of the following century, it spouted with less frequency, yet with such fury that even Geyser paled in comparison. At the time, Geyser's jets reached a height of 30 m (98 ft), whereas Strokkur would spout 40 m (131 ft). It had, however, calmed down considerably in 1830, and rarely spouted on its own accord, so people had to encourage it with stones and turf, which the spring would subsequently throw up. Thu Strokkur could be persuaded to spout, but rarely more than 20 m (66Ft). Besides, its water column was a rusty red from earth and turf. After the earthquake in 1896, it subsided completely, but rallied somewhat in 1907, yet not to its previous glorious state. By 1920 it had expired again. On the recommendation of the Geyser committee, a 40 m (131ft) deep hole was drilled from the bottom of its basin in 1963, after which it has spouted or at least squirted merrily ever since. Discharge from the spring, or rather from the borehole, is currently 2.5 l/s. (0.66 gal/s).

Because of the mini geysers in the area, you can see the steam coming out from a few areas. The scent of the steam you ask? It had a hint of sulfur. I am rather surprised the whole country did not smell of it since it was also steaming from mountainsides. The air overall smelled quite fresh.

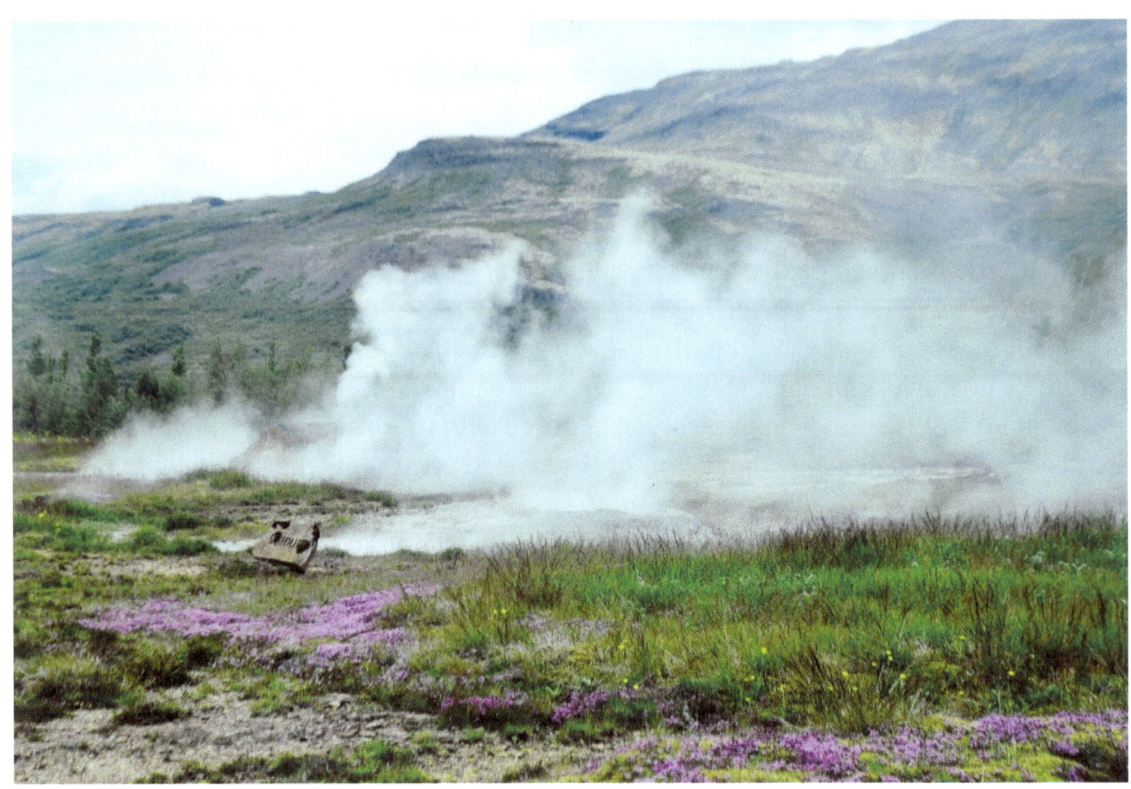

This part won't get too much information. I did not visit this portion, so can't speak for details. If interested, a place to stop from the Geyser area is Skálholt Church, which was the seat of religious power in Iceland for centuries and where some of the most dramatic events in Iceland's history took place. We did not make this stop as the group wanted to spend a little more time in the other areas.

One thing about Iceland is there is so much geothermal activity that it is harnessed as clean energy. Hellisheiði Power Plant, sitting at the foot of Mt. Hengill Volcano, is an example of that. The earth's most forces are harnessed and converted to clean energy for space heating. We did not stop; however, it was pointed out on the ride back to Reykjavík.

Located in the South of Iceland, Hellisheidarvirkjun (or Hellisheidi) heat and power plant (CHP) constitutes the largest power station of Iceland and the second largest geothermal power station in the world. The geothermal power plant was created to provide electricity to the city of Reykjavik, as there is an increasing demand. Only 11 km separate the Hellisheidarvirkjun geothermal plant from Nesjavellir, which is the second largest geothermal power in Iceland.

Hengill volcano is made from palagonite tuff and its highest point is around 800 meters above sea level. Hengill geothermal area is located in the middle of the western volcanic zone, on the plate boundary between North America and European plates. The area is one of the most powerful geothermal areas in the world with several thousand of hot springs at the surface and a giant magma chamber lying underground. Hengill volcano is still active, although its last eruption occurred about 2000 years ago.

In my opinion, for the short duration of the trip, I did not miss this. I hope to return to Iceland, and incorporate these locations then.

Note - As I was writing this, I knew a coworker had already gone to Iceland, so when we met, we started swapping stories. She went over Christmas. This is her take on a few things she saw (or wanted to see) and did:

In wanting to see the northern lights, a recommendation was to stay for 7 days to catch them. One would think that they would be out more, however, that is not the case for such reasons as too much cloud cover, atmospheric conditions not met, etc. She went independently and recommended that taking a tour to catch them would have better than going independently. On a tour, they are usually radioing each other from different spots, and those who find the northern lights give locations, and that is where people go.

Until my coworker mentioned it, I did not realize there is an option to snorkel the fissures in the Thingvellir National Park area. The waters are clear; however, she could only really see to a depth of 20 feet before it went into a total darkness. The guidelines were the jagged edges from where the fissures separated. Fish were not present, perhaps because of time of year? Speculation.

When I showed her my pictures, and she noted they were in early July, she realized how different it truly looked. She saw snow and ice. I saw green moss/grass and wild flowers. We agreed it was beautiful both ways, just different.

Note: Even though I went in summer, I still carried a raincoat and wore boots (with traction), as it was more of the damp kind of chill with potential wind and the boots came in handy for a more rugged terrain.

Food section.
I was overall too enamored by the sites to stop and take images of food. Translation, I ended up skipping lunch. Because of that, I made it a point at dinner to stop, sit back, and indulge.

I now take you to my food pictures…

Lamb tartar. It looks large, but really, it was more of an amuse bouche portion and had a bit of spicy kick to it.

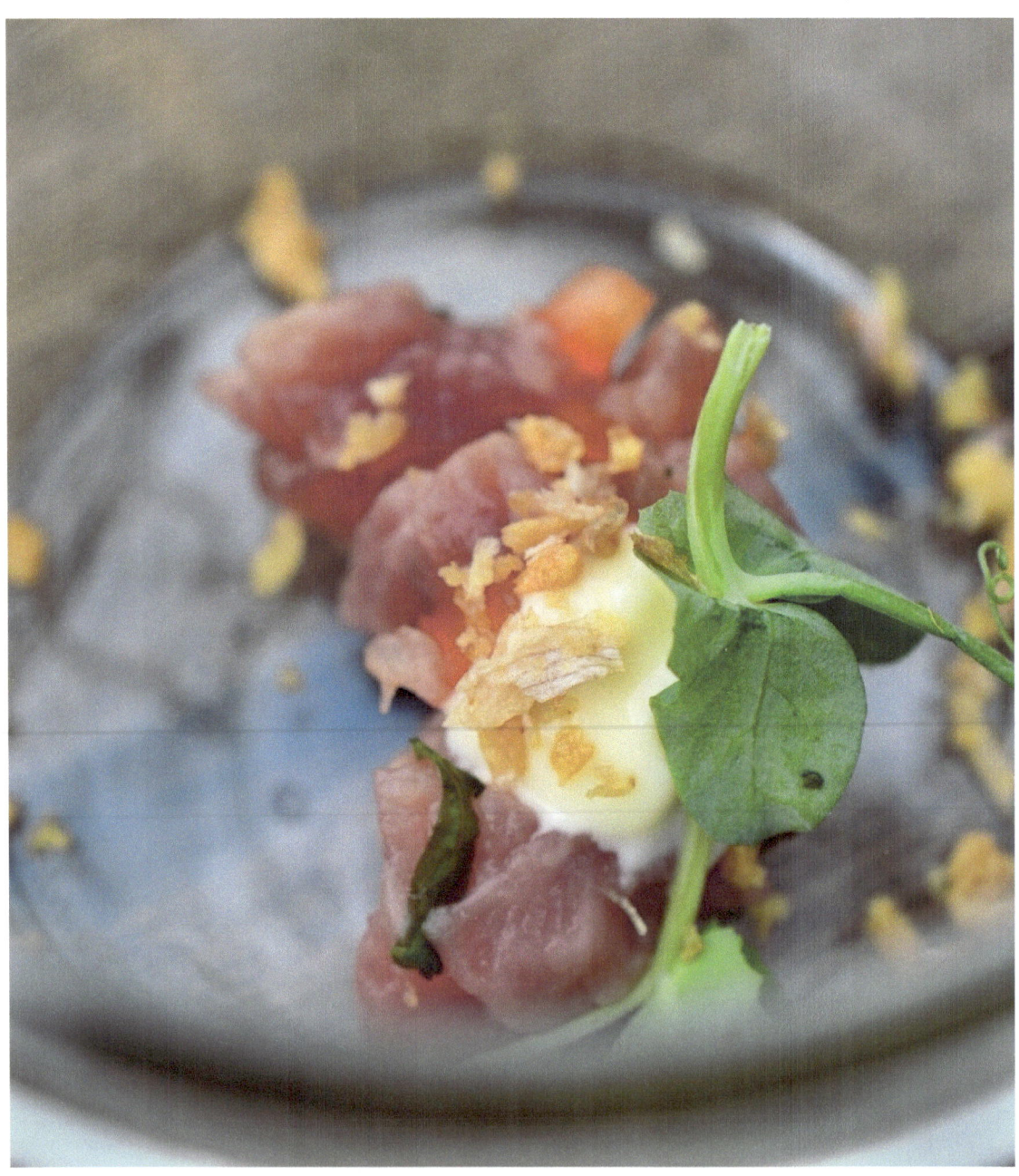

Atlantic Wolffish. It was sitting on top of smashed potatoes with carrots, beets and lightly pickled onions. This followed the lamb tartar. It was the special fish of the day at the restaurant I visited located at the marina. I had never heard of it and asked what it compared to. It was described as an Atlantic Catfish. Ok – I will take it! It did have a much firmer texture than "catfish." Other names this fish goes by: Sea Wolf, Atlantic Catfish, Ocean Catfish, Devilfish, Wolf Eel, Woof (this is not a typographical error), or Sea Cat.

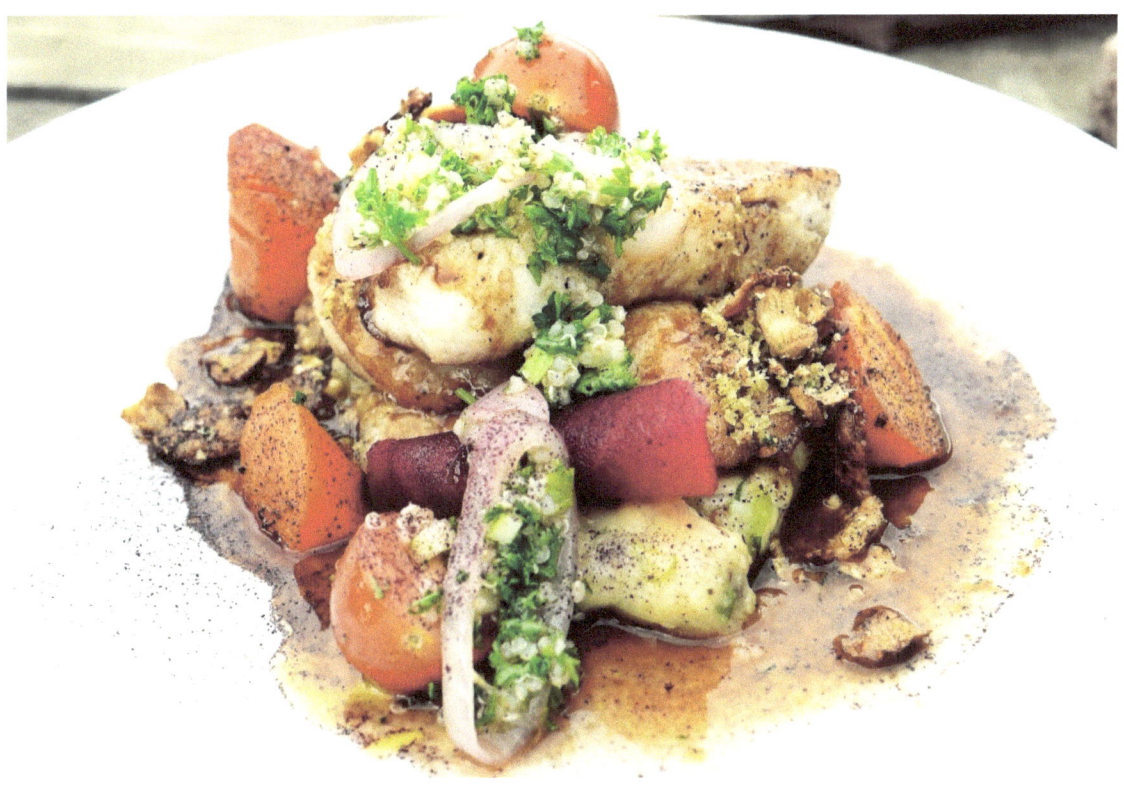

Beef Tenderloin with a mushroom puree and leeks. The mushroom puree was intense and balanced out the meat. The leeks were a perfect complement. I actually can't recall if they asked the temperature of the meat I wanted. This is how it came out - crisp on the outside, tender (and warm) on the inside.

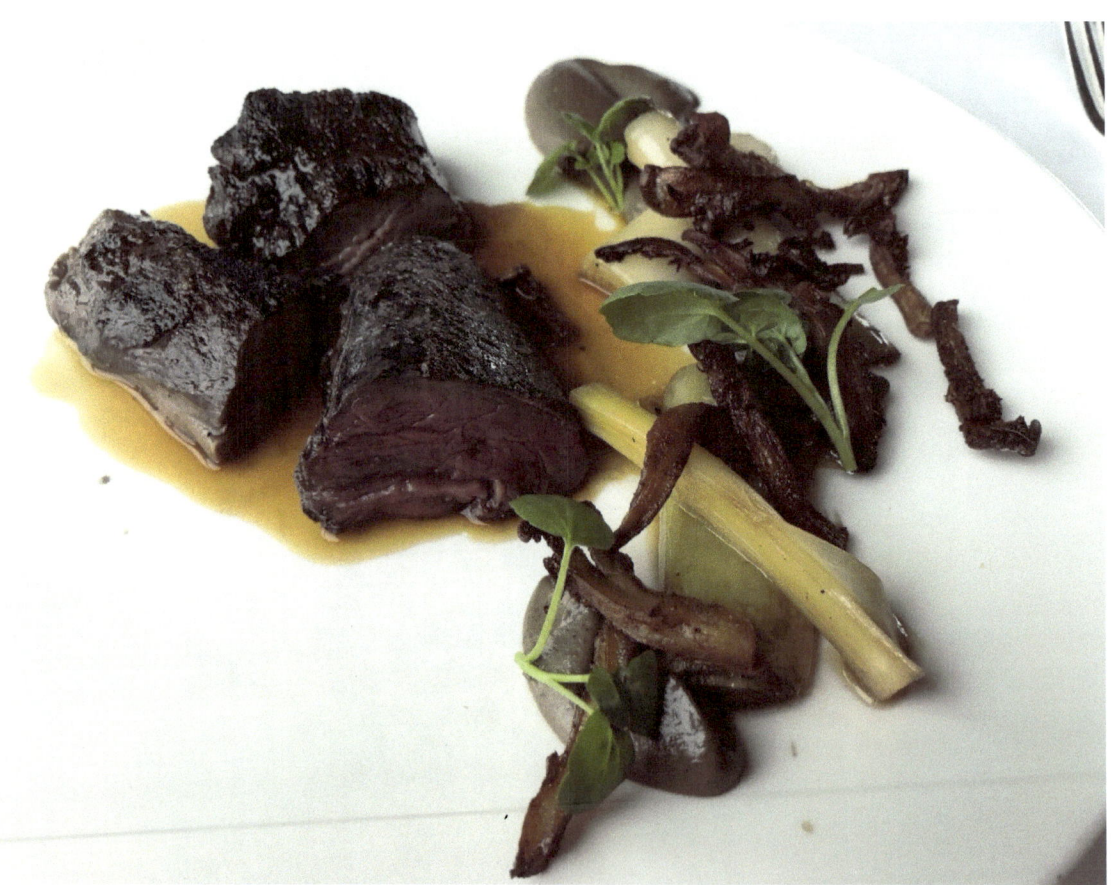

No – I did not forget dessert! ☺

This is a rhubarb cake with Ice cream, which was drizzled with salted caramel.

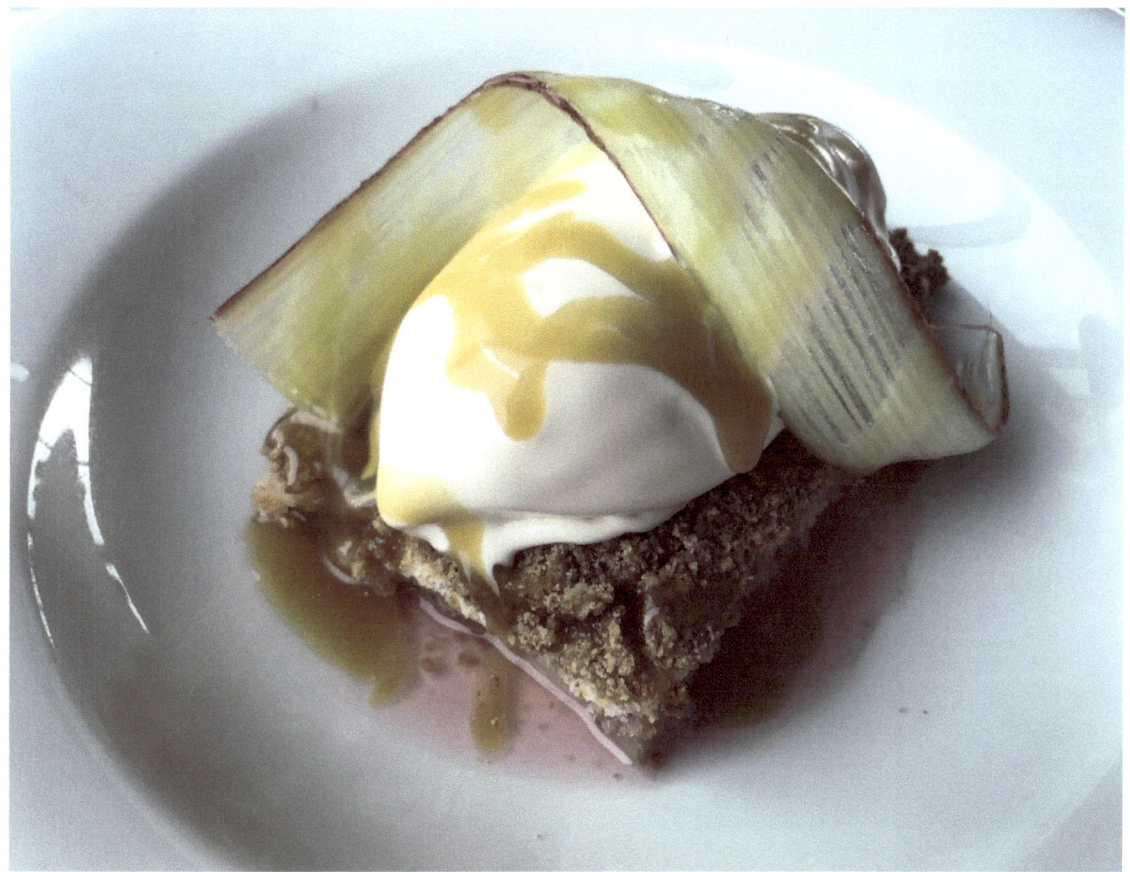

Whiskey toffee, doughnut with salted caramel, almond cake. These were not big – just a bite a piece.

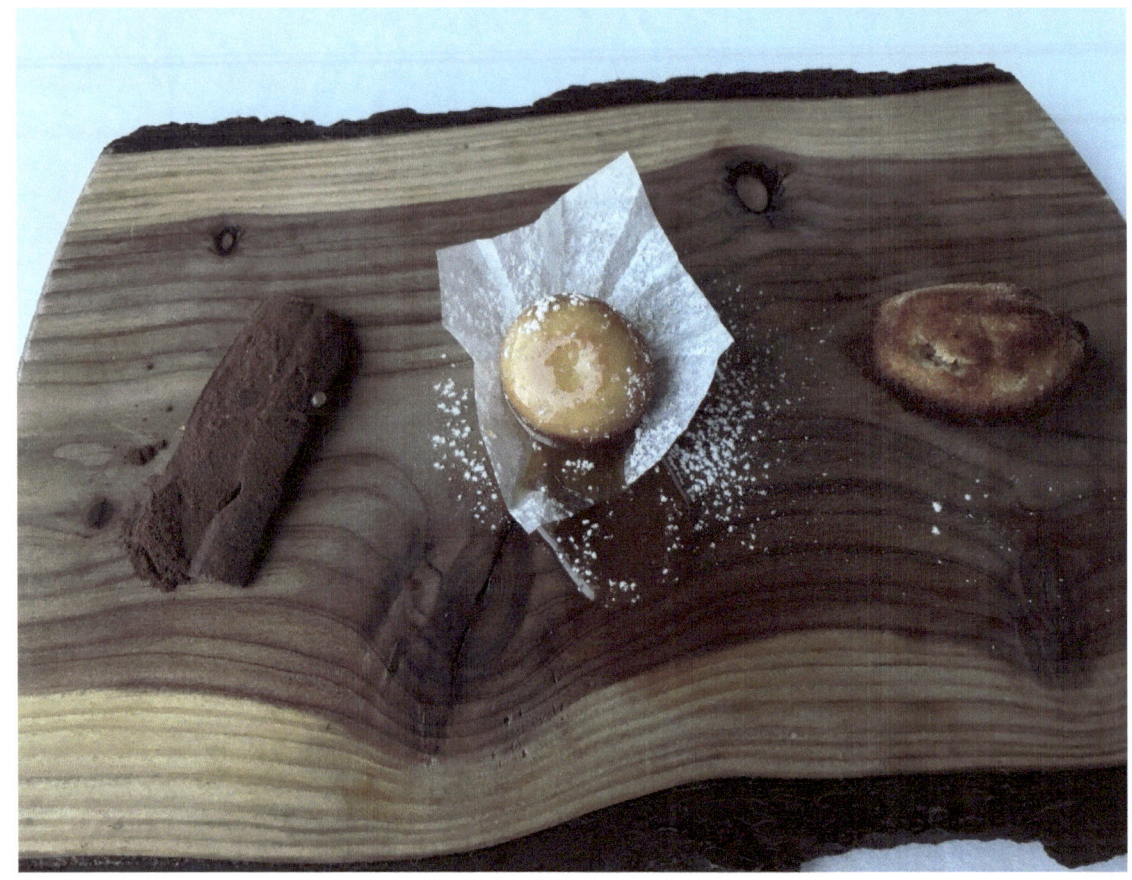

Icelandic licorice. I thought these had a stronger anise taste than the American counterpart and thought I tasted coconut in them as well, in particular the pieces which had the white, green, and/or pink color. Apparently, tourists don't like the taste of these; I was a different story though. I liked them and brought some back home to share. The staff at the hotel and I were eating this batch together.

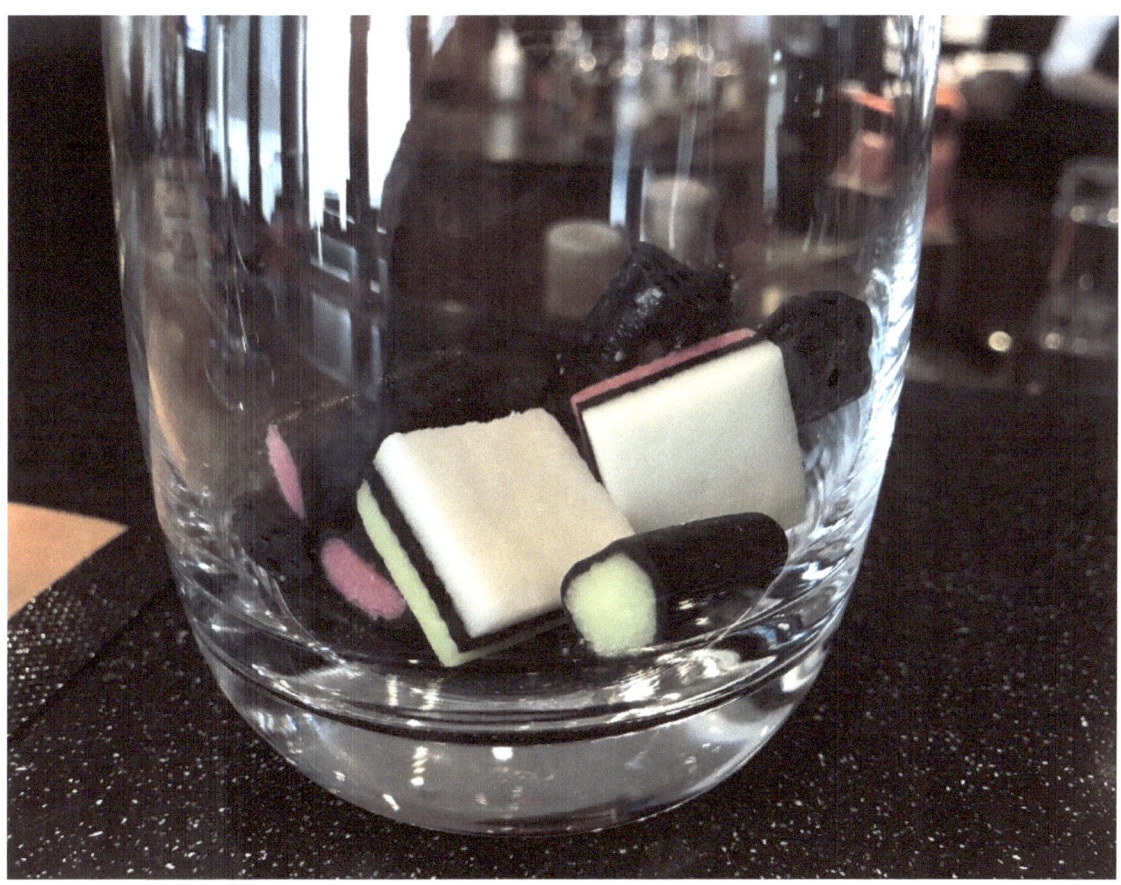

In retrospection, I would have planned some parts of this trip differently. I was in Iceland, for 3 days using Reykjavík as my hub.
1. I should have switched the Golden Circle tour on Day 3 with the Blue Lagoon on Day 2. I felt the Blue Lagoon was more leisurely with more options to come back earlier. I generally prefer more leisurely last days as it helps me unwind before the trip back.
2. If I planned one more day, I would have gone to see the glaciers where there is an option to visit a glacier cave.
3. Unfortunately, my hotel, although close to Reykjavík city proper, was not as easily walkable to restaurants and the like. It would have made for a much nicer stroll before and/or after dinner. The in-town hotels booked a lot faster, so I should have booked sooner or looked into a pension. This is a result of huge amounts of tourism, which Iceland is seeing overall.

A few tidbits about Iceland:
1. There are over 300 types of moss.
2. There are no snakes or mosquitos.
3. Some of their animals include Icelandic horses, sheep, arctic fox, and puffin.
4. About a third of the population lives in Reykjavik.
5. Did you notice from the pictures there weren't a lot of trees? That wasn't intentional for me to not get them. Moss and wildflowers dominated.

To show where I concentrated my time, here are some of the pin drops to the locations I visited:

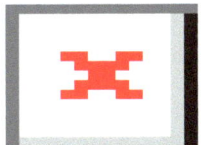

Acknowledgements:

This trip was booked as an independent trip through Gate1 travels. Gate1 set up the hotel (there were multiple options reflecting different grades), the optional tours, and the air travel.

Optional tours were provided by Gray Line Iceland and Reykjavik Excursions.
Stories and information on the sites provided by tour guides.
Map generated using TripAdvisor/Google software.

www.ingramcontent.com/pod-product-compliance
Lightning Source LLC
Chambersburg PA
CBHW051820210526
45473CB00005B/1677